NATIONAL GEOGRAPHIC

Ladders

Common Core Readers

Moon Mysteries

The Sock Sneak Mystery

by Renee Biermann
illustrated by Laura Perez

NARRATOR 1

NARRATOR 2

ANDRE
male summer camper

TYLER
male summer camper

LUCIA
female summer camper

GRACE
female summer camper

EMMA
female camp counselor

JASPER
male camp counselor

WES
male camp counselor

2

INTRODUCTION

[**SETTING** *The play takes place at Black Lake Summer Camp.*
NARRATOR 1 and NARRATOR 2 enter and speak to the audience.
They both show excitement.]

NARRATOR 1: Welcome to Black Lake Summer Camp!

NARRATOR 2: This summer, something amazing happened
that had never happened before.

NARRATOR 1: Someone solved a very dark mystery.

NARRATOR 2: What mystery, you ask? A very dark,
sneaky mystery, indeed.

NARRATOR 1 and **NARRATOR 2:** [*look at each other,*
then say together] The mystery of the Sock Sneak!

NARRATOR 1: What's a Sock
Sneak, you ask??

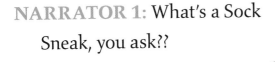

NARRATOR 2: A Sock Sneak is a sneaky person who steals socks.

NARRATOR 1: Why would someone steal socks?

NARRATOR 2: Socks are stolen for FUN! Each year, a counselor at Black Lake Summer Camp steals socks from the campers.

NARRATOR 1: For many years, no one knew who the Sock Sneak was.

NARRATOR 2: The campers never knew when the Sock Sneak would strike, so there was an annual competition to see who could figure it out.

NARRATOR 1: All of that changed this year, however, when a certain clue shed light on the mystery . . . by not shedding light!

NARRATOR 2: Let's see how it all started . . .

ACT 1

[**SETTING** *At Black Lake Summer Camp, EMMA, JASPER, and WES are standing in front of the campers. ANDRE, LUCIA, GRACE, and TYLER are sitting nearby, listening with interest.*]

JASPER: Listen up, campers! It's time for the annual Sock Sneak Competition.

EMMA: [*teasing*] I don't know, guys. We've seen quite a few socks run up the flagpole over the years.

WES: It's true, campers. At some phase during your two-week stay, one of us will steal your socks and run them up the flagpole. It's your job to figure out when this will happen.

JASPER: If you solve the mystery, you'll win a special prize.

EMMA: There has been a Sock Sneak at this camp for 10 years, but no one has figured it out. Can you?

JASPER: [*points to himself*] Will *I* sneak *Monday?*

WES: [*points to himself*] Will *I* sneak *Tuesday?*

EMMA: [*points to herself*] Will *I* sneak *Wednesday?*

JASPER: Good luck, campers. I hope the time will come when one of you can solve this dark mystery. In the meantime, let's go swimming!

[JASPER *and* WES *walk offstage.* ANDRE, TYLER, *and* GRACE *look excited to go swimming and get up to walk to the beach.* LUCIA *looks quizzically at* EMMA. EMMA *has stopped to pretend to tie her shoe.* LUCIA *hides behind a bush to watch* EMMA. NARRATOR 1 *and* NARRATOR 2 *enter. They stand on the edge of the stage to address the audience.*]

NARRATOR 1: Lucia saw Emma lean down to tie her shoe, but it was already laced.

NARRATOR 2: What was Emma doing? Lucia wanted to find out!

NARRATOR 1: Lucia's friends went to the beach, but she waited behind a bush to see what Emma would do next.

NARRATOR 2: [*looks at NARRATOR 1*] Lucia is very clever.

NARRATOR 1: [*looks at NARRATOR 2 and nods*] Yes, very clever.

[EMMA *stands up. She pulls a piece of folded paper from her pocket and reads it.*]

EMMA: [*speaking to herself*] Hmm . . . . That's right!

[LUCIA *looks confused. She's still watching from behind the bush.* EMMA *goes to put the piece of paper back in her pocket, but she drops it. As* EMMA *walks away,* LUCIA *runs out and snatches the paper.*]

NARRATOR 1: Lucia didn't know what was on that piece of paper, but she thought it could be a clue.

NARRATOR 2: She was correct.

LUCIA: [*speaking to herself*] Very sneaky!

[LUCIA *looks happy and runs to catch up with her friends at the beach.*]

ACT 2

[**SETTING** It's later that night, and the campers have gathered to talk.]

GRACE: I really want to win the Sock Sneak Competition, but I don't know when the Sneak will strike.

ANDRE: I feel the same way. Every year, I try to guess, but I'm always wrong.

TYLER: It'll probably be sometime next week. That's my guess.

LUCIA: [*confident*] I know when the Sock Sneak will strike.

GRACE: What's your guess?

LUCIA: It's not a guess, I figured it out. I know when it will happen.

TYLER: [*doubtful*] Oh yeah, Lucia? When?

LUCIA: It's going to happen tonight.

[TYLER, ANDRE, *and* GRACE
look surprised.]

TYLER: Tonight?

LUCIA: Yes, tonight, and it's going to be Emma!

ANDRE: No way!

GRACE: How do you know?

LUCIA: I'll give you a little clue. It has to do with
something "**waxing.**"

TYLER: Is someone waxing the dining room floor?

ANDRE: Is someone waxing the camp bus?

LUCIA: [*laughs*] No. Here is another clue. It has to do with something "**waning.**"

GRACE: Did you say "raining"? It's not raining.

LUCIA: [*smiling at GRACE*] No, silly. I said "WANING."

[*GRACE, TYLER, and ANDRE all look hopelessly confused.*]

LUCIA: Think about it carefully. There has to be some kind of pattern that the Sock Sneak follows.

TYLER: So the Sock Sneak would do the same thing each year?

ANDRE: Yeah, there has to be a pattern.

GRACE: [*angry*] I still don't know what this has to do with raining because it's not raining!

LUCIA: [*amused*] Oh, Grace, I'm not talking about the weather. Come on. I'll show you.

11

ACT 3

[**SETTING** *Pathway near the flagpole. GRACE, LUCIA, ANDRE, and TYLER are hiding behind the bushes waiting for EMMA. They are cramped together and are all peeking toward the path.*]

GRACE: Why are we hiding in the bushes?

LUCIA: We're going to catch Emma the Sock Sneak.

ANDRE: Are you sure she's coming?

TYLER: [*frustrated*] Shhh! We don't want anyone to hear us.

[TYLER *moves closer to the group and steps on GRACE'S foot.*]

GRACE: Ouch, Tyler, you're standing on my foot!

TYLER: Sorry, Grace!

ANDRE: Quiet!

EMMA: [*surprised*] ACK! [*laughs*] I've finally been discovered!

[*Everyone laughs. LUCIA, GRACE, TYLER, and ANDRE help EMMA pick up the socks.*]

EMMA: Which one of you figured it out?

ANDRE: It was Lucia.

GRACE: I still don't understand what this has to do with "waxing" or "raining" . . . I mean "waning."

LUCIA: Those clues were about the **lunar** calendar. The moon has **phases,** and it can be waxing or waning.

TYLER: But tonight's a **new moon,** so we cannot see it!

LUCIA: I know. That's how I knew tonight would be the night the Sock Sneak struck. When there's a new moon, it's very dark outside.

GRACE: I understand now! The Sock Sneak strikes when there's a new moon so that no one can see her!

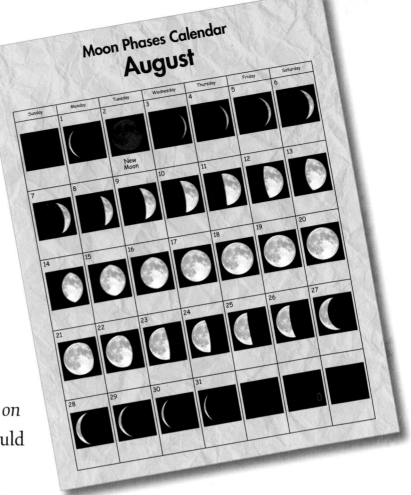

LUCIA: Exactly! I saw Emma drop this piece of paper today.

[LUCIA *pulls out piece of paper and unfolds it. It's a lunar calendar for July.*]

LUCIA: Today is the new moon. [*points to new moon on calendar*] I knew Emma would be at the flagpole tonight because it would be so dark.

EMMA: I'm so proud of you, Lucia. Good job! You win the prize!

[EMMA *pulls a special, colorful flag out of her pocket. She takes a marker and writes "LUCIA" on the flag. Then she runs the flag up the flagpole.*]

[JASPER *and* WES *come running up to the flagpole.*]

JASPER: [*worried*] What's all the commotion about?

WES: [*anxious*] We heard you yelling!

EMMA: Everyone is fine. Lucia caught me sneaking out here with the socks!

[*Everyone cheers.*]

[NARRATOR 1 *and* NARRATOR 2 *enter.*]

NARRATOR 1: And that is how the Sock Sneak mystery was solved at Black Lake Summer Camp.

NARRATOR 2: The end.

[NARRATOR 1 *and* NARRATOR 2 *bow.*]

Check In   How does Lucia solve the mystery?

OBSERVING THE MOON

by Nate George

Moon, Earth, and Sun

The moon is a **sphere,** or a ball. It **revolves,** or moves around, Earth. One trip around Earth takes about one month. Earth and the moon also revolve around the sun.

The moon does not give off its own light. It reflects light from the sun. "Moonlight" is sunlight that has bounced off the moon.

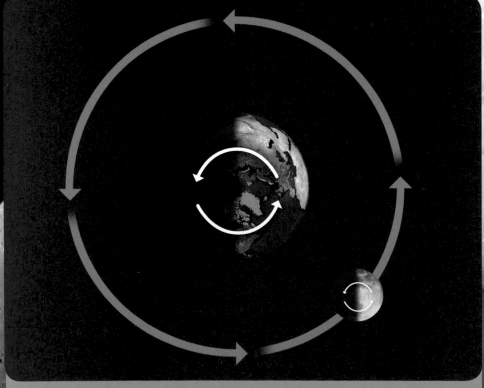

The blue arrows show that the moon revolves around Earth.
The white arrows show that Earth and the moon also rotate, or spin.

A **full moon** occurs when Earth is between the sun and the moon. During a full moon, you see the entire sunlit half of the moon. When you face a full moon, where is the sun?

A **new moon** occurs when the moon is between the sun and Earth. During a new moon, you can't see the sunlit half of the moon.

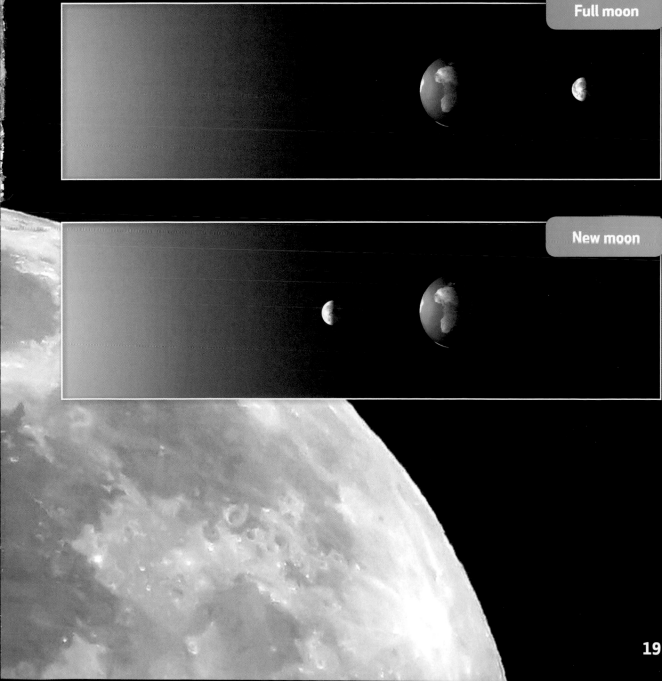

Full moon

New moon

Phases of the Moon

The moon can look like a circle, a half circle, or even a banana. The shape of the moon seems to change over time. Each shape is a **phase** of the moon.

The sun lights the half of the moon that faces it. As the moon revolves around Earth, you see different parts of the sunlit half. You might see all of it. That's a full moon. You might see part of it. That could be a crescent moon, a quarter moon, or a gibbous moon. If you don't see any of it, that's a new moon.

The phases change in a pattern. When the moon is **waxing,** you see more of its sunlit half. When the moon is **waning,** you see less of it. The time from one new moon to the next new moon is about one month.

Phases of the Moon

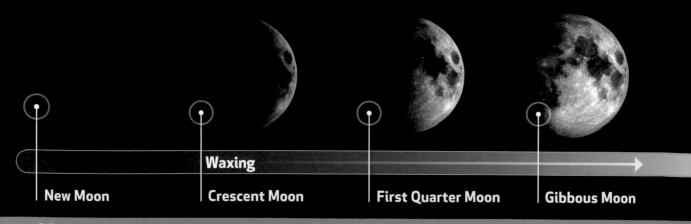

Waxing

New Moon | Crescent Moon | First Quarter Moon | Gibbous Moon

Why a Quarter Moon?

Look at the first quarter moon. During this phase, the moon looks like half of a circle. So why is this phase called a *quarter moon?* Remember, the moon revolves around Earth. When you see the moon in this phase, it has finished one quarter of its trip around Earth. That's why this phase is called a *quarter moon.*

The moon can be seen sometimes during the day and sometimes at night.

Waning

Full Moon **Gibbous Moon** **Last Quarter Moon** **Crescent Moon**

Lunar Eclipses

A **lunar eclipse** occurs when Earth's shadow falls on the moon. Remember, a full moon occurs when Earth is between the sun and the moon. Full moons are usually a bit above or below Earth's shadow. But sometimes, a full moon falls in Earth's shadow. This causes a lunar eclipse. The diagram shows what happens during a lunar eclipse.

You can still see the moon during a lunar eclipse. Its color changes from gray to dark red.

A total lunar eclipse occurs when Earth's shadow covers all of the sunlit half of the moon. A partial lunar eclipse occurs when Earth's shadow covers part of it.

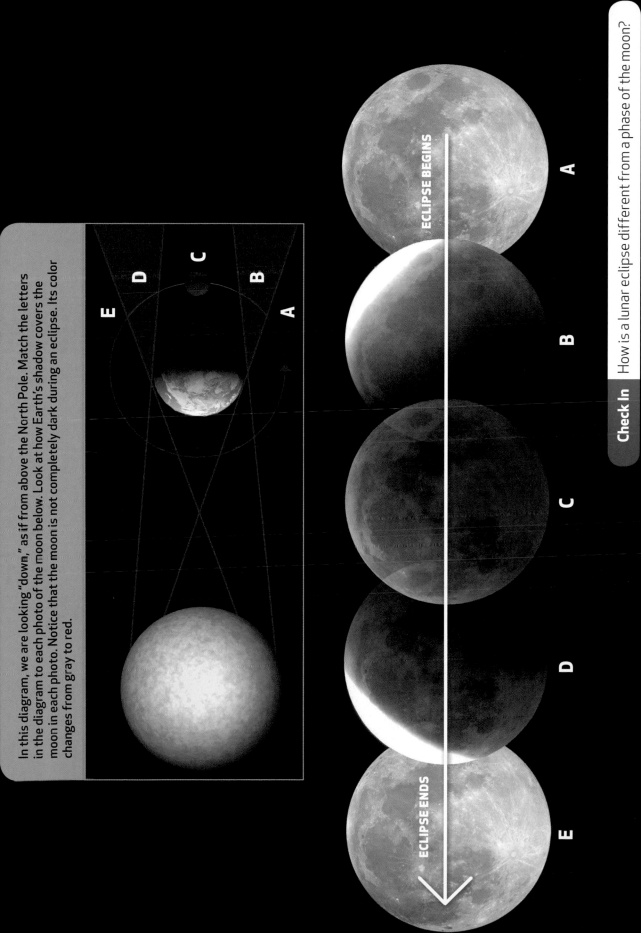

In this diagram, we are looking "down," as if from above the North Pole. Match the letters in the diagram to each photo of the moon below. Look at how Earth's shadow covers the moon in each photo. Notice that the moon is not completely dark during an eclipse. Its color changes from gray to red.

E   D   C

          B

A

ECLIPSE BEGINS

ECLIPSE ENDS

A   B   C   D   E

Check In   How is a lunar eclipse different from a phase of the moon?

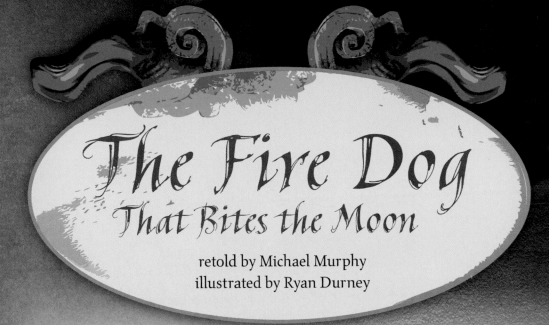

The Fire Dog
That Bites the Moon

retold by Michael Murphy
illustrated by Ryan Durney

People have told folk tales to explain the mysteries of the moon for years. Some tales tell why the moon **waxes** and **wanes** during its **phases.** Others tell why a **new moon** looks dark. This Korean tale is one way to explain a partial lunar eclipse.

Once there was an underground country of **caverns** called the Land of Darkness. The only light in these caverns was firelight. People there used strong Fire Dogs to carry sticks and logs to keep the fires burning.

The king worried that his country was still too dark. He heard tales of great lights in the sky, the sun and the moon. He wondered if a Fire Dog could capture one of those lights for the Land of Darkness.

The king **summoned** his fiercest Fire Dog. He told it to
leap into the sky, **seize** the sun, and bring it back. So the dog
raced through the caverns until it reached the end of the Land
of Darkness. There, light streamed in through a big opening.

Then the fiercest Fire Dog took a huge leap. It flew higher and higher into the sky. It went closer and closer to the sun. But then, lo and behold, it was forced to stop. The sun was just too hot. The fiercest Fire Dog could not get close enough to the sun to steal it. So the fiercest Fire Dog returned to the caverns without the light for the king.

The king did not give up. He decided that moonlight would be better than firelight alone. So he summoned his next-fiercest Fire Dog and told it to leap into the sky, seize the moon, and bring it back to the Land of Darkness.

So the second-fiercest Fire Dog took a huge leap. It flew higher and higher into the sky. It went closer and closer to the moon. Then, lo and behold, it reached the moon!

Alas, when the second-fiercest Fire Dog tried to bite the moon, it froze the dog's mouth! Still, this dog was **tenacious.** It did not give up. It bit the moon again and again. Each time the dog swallowed more of the moon.

But in the end, the Fire Dog had to spit the moon out. And so the second-fiercest Fire Dog returned to the caverns of the Land of Darkness without the light for the king.

Despite these two failed efforts, the king never gave up hope. Again and again, the king ordered his second-fiercest Fire Dog to seize the moon and bring it back.

Yet again and again, the tenacious Fire Dog could not complete its task. It had to spit out the ice-cold moon. So the Land of Darkness stayed dark and the king never got his light.

Ever since, people have told this story. They say the dark part of the moon during a lunar eclipse is the bite of the tenacious Fire Dog.

Check In How does this folk tale explain a partial lunar eclipse?

Discuss Text Structure and Concepts

1. Explain the differences between a play and a story. What elements does a play have that a story does not have?

2. How do the visuals in the folk tale help tell the story?

3. What is happening when there is a full moon? Explain.

4. What is happening when there is a new moon? Explain.

5. What questions do you still have about moon phases and eclipses? What else would you like to know?